Bargello Needlepoint Guideline For Beginners

Basic Technique and Things Related to Bargello Needlepoint

DEDICATION

Contents

Bargello (Needlework)

Bargello is a type of needlepoint embroidery consisting of upright flat stitches laid in a mathematical pattern to create motifs. The name originates from a series of chairs found in the Bargello palace in Florence, which have a "flame stitch" pattern.

Traditionally, Bargello was stitched in wool on canvas. Embroidery done this way is remarkably durable. It is well suited for use on pillows, upholstery and even carpets, but not for clothing. In most traditional pieces, all stitches are vertical with stitches going over two or more threads.

Traditional designs are very colourful, and use many hues of one colour, which produces intricate shading effects. The patterns are naturally geometric, but can also resemble very stylised flowers or fruits. Bargello is considered particularly challenging, as it requires very precise counting of squares for the mathematical pattern connected with the various motifs to accurately execute designs

What is bargello?

In Bargello, distinctive patterns are built up from rows of straight stitches, arranged in a zigzag line, and repeated in varying shades or colors.

The steepness of the zigzag depends on how many threads the stitch

is worked over, and the position of subsequent stitches. The diagram below shows that when the stitches are stepped by more canvas threads the peak is higher.

To give a more rounded effect groups of stitches can be worked either at the end or part way down a slope, as in the photo at the bottom of this page. Traditionally all the stitches in a design are the same length throughout.

They can also be arranged to form a lattice work, as in the photo, above

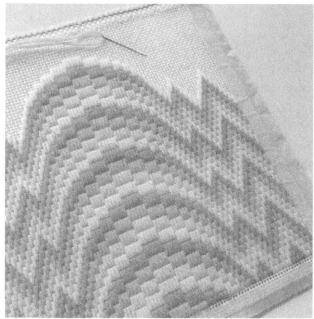

Alternative names

A number of alternative names are used by different scholars, including:

Florentine work - After the fact that the Bargello Museum is in Florence.

Hungarian point (punto unghero) - In Italian, Bargello is known as "Hungarian Point" (Williams 1967: 5, Petschek 1997), indicating that the Florentines believed the technique originated in Hungary. However, English embroidery vocabulary also includes a diamond-shaped stitch called the Hungarian point, so few English-language books use this term to refer to Bargello.

Flame stitch (punto fiamma) - A type of Bargello motif in which zig-zag or flames are created. The chairs in the Bargello museum do use flame stitch motifs, but curved motifs are also common (see below). These curved Bargello motifs would normally not be "flame stitch", but would be called Bargello.

Because of the potential for confusion, most books written in English refer to the technique simply as "Bargello" (Williams 1969, Kaestner 1972, Petscheck 1997).

History of Bargello Needlepoint

As with many traditional crafts, the origins of Bargello are not well documented. Although early examples are from the Bargello Museum in Florence, there does exist documentation that a Hungarian connection is possible. For one thing, the Bargello Museum inventory identifies the chairs in its inventory as "17th century with backs and seats done in punto unghero (Hungarian Point)." (Williams, 1967:5). In the 18th century, Queen Maria Teresa of Hungary stitched Bargello and her work has been preserved in the Hungarian National Museum

Petschek (1997:7) also cites additional "legends" of Hungarian noblewomen practicing the craft, including a Hungarian princess marrying into the de Medici family, and a princess Jadwiga (Hedwig) of Hungary who married into the Jagiełło dynasty of Poland.

It is unknown if those were distinct developments or if they influenced each other. Both Bargello and Hungarian Point tend to be colorful and use many hues of one color, which produces intricate shading effects. The patterns are naturally geometric, but can also resemble very stylized flowers or fruits.

Basic Bargello Technique

Bargello refers not to just a stitching technique, but also to motifs created by the change of colors in the stitches. This section describes the vertical stitch, and how it is combined with color and "stepping" to create different motifs.

Vertical stitches

Most agree that traditional Bargello pieces incorporate a series of all vertical stitches (vs. diagonal stitches). The basic unit is usually a vertical stitch of four threads, but other heights are possible.

Some Bargello pieces use only one height of stitch, but even the earliest pieces (such as chairs in the Bargello museum) combine different heights of stitches.

Stepping

Bargello patterns are formed when vertical stitches are stepped or offset vertically, usually by two threads (i.e., halfway down a unit of four threads). The patterns in the steps combined with color changes determines how the overall pattern will emerge.

Flame (sharp) vs. curved motifs

If vertical stitches are stepped down quickly, the design forms sharp points or zig-zags. This type of Bargello motif is often known as "flame stitch". Flame stitch can be found on the Bargello Museum chairs.

If steps are gradual, then the design will appear to be curved. Traditional curved Bargello motifs include medallions and ribbons.

Examples of Bargello motifs

6

There are many identified motifs possible (Williams 1967), but some common ones include:

Flame zigzag (sharp)
Stitches step sharply across the design. xd
Diamonds (sharp)
Stitches step sharply across the designs and color changes cause diamonds to appear.

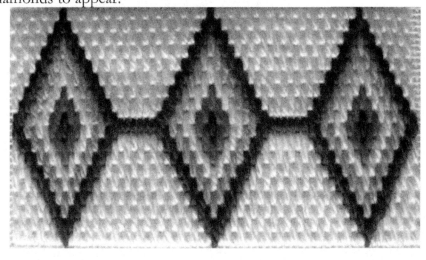

Example of diamond motif formed with Bargello stitches. Image created and licensed by Elizabeth Pyatt.

Ribbonsri (curved)
Stitches are gradually stepped in different colors.

Medallions (curved)
Stitches are gradually stepped and color changes cause spheres or medallions to appear.

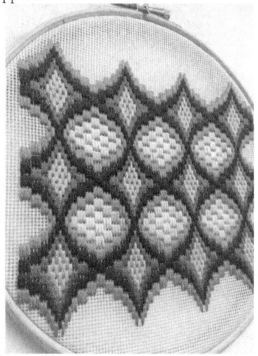

Modern Bargello
Since the revival of Bargello in the 1960s, the technique has evolved in different directions. Although traditional Bargello is still stitched, modern designers have expanded the repertoire of design possibilities.

Four-way and eight-way Bargello

Traditional Bargello is executed with just a vertical stitch in one direction, but Dorothy Kaestner (1972) created a style of Bargello called four-way Bargello. In this technique, the canvas is first divided diagonally into quarters. Then the same motif is worked in horizontal stitches in two opposite areas, and vertical stitches in the remaining two areas. The resulting design frequently resembles a kaleidoscope effect.

Kaestner describes the origin of the technique:

My first piece of four-way Bargello was started approximately ten years ago [in the early 1960s]. I placed a mirror on a Bargello design in a way that showed me how it would look if I mitered [turned] a corner. This intrigued me so much, I graphed a design starting in the center and mitering all four corners.

Some examples include

- Cathy Decker
- Stan Taylor
- Stan Taylor

This concept has been expanded to eight-way Bargello, or Bargello stitches in eight directions (horizontal stitches, vertical stitches and diagonal stitches), by designers including Susan Kerndt:

- Kaleidoscope (Eight Way Bargello by Susan Kerndt)
- Ice Crystals (Eight Way Bargello by Susan Kerndt)

The two links above are broken so try the alternative link below for samples of Susan Kerndt's work, including Kaleidoscope and Ice Crystal

Bargello band samplers

Designers of band samplers may include a band of a Bargello motif among other sampler stitches. Unlike traditional Bargello, these bands are stitched with the same stranded cotton, silk or linen embroidery thread used in band samplers.

Bargello quilts

In addition to Bargello embroidery, there are now Bargello quilts in which the patterns used in Bargello embroidery are constructed with strips of fabric of the same height but different widths.

In Bargello quilting, long strips of fabric are sewn together along their long sides. Then the first and last strip are sewn together, forming a loop. The loop is laid flat on a table, and then cut vertically (in the opposite direction from how the strips were sewn together) to make many narrow loops. The quilter then opens the loops by pulling out the stitching between two pieces of fabric, making a long, flat strip. Finally, all the strips are sewn together. By opening the loops in between different pieces of fabric (for instance, between the first and second piece on one loop, then the second and third piece on the next loop), the artist can make the colors of the quilt appear to shift and wave. Slicing the loops very narrowly makes the waving and movement appear sharp and fast; cutting wide loops creates more gentle movement in the quilt.

Patterns of Bargello embroidery are made up of vertical adjacent stitches, whose lenght may be fixed or vary. Only the straight stitch is used. Traditionally, it is executed in two ways: stitches of different lengths, staggered from each other by two or three holes of the canvas (called Hungarian point), or in a 4:2 step pattern, with stitches of four threads vertically staggered by two holes (Florentine stitch, alsto called Flame Stitch).

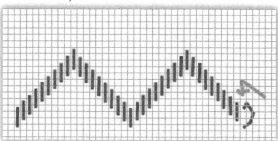

This kind of embroidery starts from the center of the canvas and is executed in stripes up and down from the starting row, from left to right or from right to left. No more counting is necessary because all other rows follow the first row.

Only the colors may vary from row to row, while all stitches are vertical. The stitches cover all the surface of the canvas, which is rigid and with its large holes works as a guide for the embroidery. In the past, these kinds of canvas were used as dusters and for that reason they could be used also to do embroidery tests.

Embroidery has always been used as a decoration, and during the years, patient women armed with needle and thread, have been creating clothings and furniture covers.

Bargello embroidery is a counted needlepoint, whose origins date back to the fifteenth century. It was probably imported from Hungary, and its name comes from the Bargello palace in Florence, former prison and palace of justice.

It has been a very common technique, either in the tiny workshops in Florence, either in women's convents or colleges. This technique has been handed down from generation to generation, transforming into a family tradition to the extent that it has become one of the most widely appreciated Florentine handicrafts. Traditionally it was used for covering furniture but it is also applicable for cushions or arazzi.

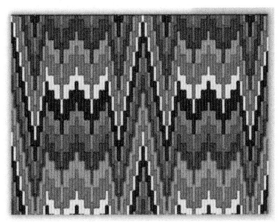

The traditional Bargello stitch (or Florentine stitch or Flame Stitch) consists of geometrically shaped patterns, like zig zag patterns (which resemble a flame) or diamonds. (look at the images below, photo taken from wikipedia.org) Usually the embroidery is made on canvas with quite thin woolen thread and is worked in several shades of different colours, going from light to dark and from dark to light, creating shadow or depth. The choice of the colors and of the stitches length is very important for the end result of the work.

Design in Bargello

There are three main types of design in this type of needlepoint: row, motif or mitered.

The simplest is a row design. The pattern is established in the first row, and then repeated using a different color, tone or tint in subsequent rows. I will explain the color terms shortly.

To create a motif design, part of a row is mirrored and a medallion or motif is formed. The medallion can be filled in repeating rows or each enclosed area can be dealt with differently. The pattern is mainly formed by the use of color.

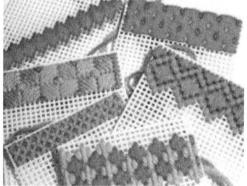

A mitered or four-way bargello needlework design consists of a triangular section that is then mirrored both ways. Both rows and motifs can be worked in this manner. Some traditional patterns worked in this way are known as tulip, rose and pineapple.

How to use color

In Bargello the pattern relies heavily on hue changes. These can be subtle or vibrant.

One color scheme you can use is monochromatic. This uses tones of one color. Take pink for example, you could start the sequence with a burgundy (a shade is made by mixing black with the original colour) and then use lighter and lighter tints (mixed with white) ending up with a very pale pink, similar to that in the photo below. This sequence is then repeated.

I don't want to get too technical here, but I'll introduce another color term; analogous. Basically this scheme uses related hues that are close to each other on the color wheel. For example red, orange and yellow. Another choice would be purple, blue and green.

Bargello needlepoint can also be worked with contrasting or complementary colors. To find any color's contrast look opposite it on the color wheel. Yellow is opposite purple and therefore its contrast. The same goes for orange and blue. The trick here is to use much less of the contrast than the main color. Think of it as an accent. If you use equal amounts of each the effect won't be as vibrant. Think of a mainly blue room that has the occasional orange pillow to give it some "spark"!

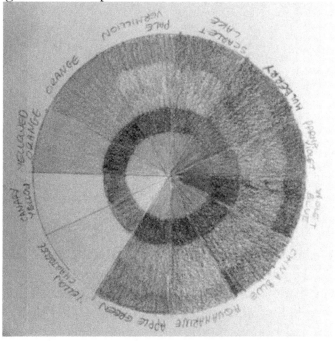

I created the color wheel above using Prismacolor colored pencils. Around the edge I pressed harder to give the most vibrant color, and the lighter color inside that represents the color with white added, or a paler tint of the original hue.

The darker inner wheel shows where I used the complementary color to "grey" the pure color, by mixing the two together (or in this case layering one over the other).

How to Do Needlepoint

Needlepoint is an enjoyable hobby that you can take anywhere and it only requires the use of a few basic types of stitches. Create designs on a painted or blank canvas, and then turn your designs into a new decorative item. You can make key chains, belts, pillows, bookmarks, stockings, belt buckles, or almost anything with your needlepoint designs.

Part 1 of 3:

1

Choose a canvas and mounting materials. Visit a craft supply store to find a canvas and a frame or stretcher bars and tacks. You can purchase a blank canvas if you plan to draw your own needlepoint design onto it, or you can buy a canvas that already has a design printed on it. Choose a frame that will be large enough to hold your canvas.[1]

A premade needlepoint design is the best option if you are new to needlepoint.

2

Bind the edges of your canvas with masking tape. Always wash your hands before you touch the canvas to avoid getting any dirt or grime onto it. This will keep the edges from unraveling while you work. Use 1 in (2.5 cm) wide or smaller tape. Fold the tape along the edges of the canvas to cover them completely from end to end.

You can also hem the edges of the canvas with a sewing machine to prevent them from unraveling.

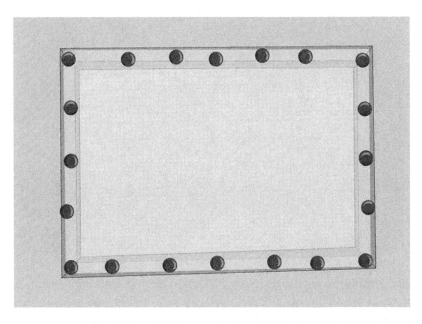

3

Mount the canvas in a frame to hold it taut while you work. Unscrew the edges of the frame and place 1 piece onto a flat surface, such as a table. Lay the canvas on the frame and tug the edges of the canvas to open it up completely. Then, place the other side of the frame over the top of the canvas and secure the pieces together to hold the canvas taut.

You can also use stretcher bars and tacks to secure your canvas.

Avoid working on loose canvas. This may increase your chances of distorting the fabric when you pull stitches taut.

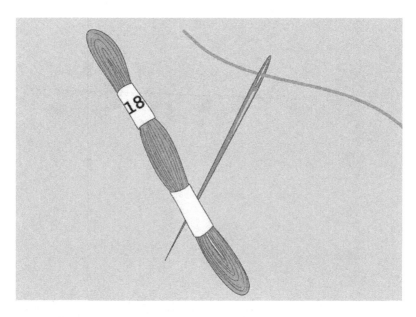

4

Thread a needle with an 18 in (46 cm) length of embroidery floss.
Hold the thread in one hand and the needle in the other (eye up).
Then, insert the tip of the thread into the eye of the needle and pull it
through by about 4 in (10 cm).[2]

You can use any type of embroidery floss, thread, or yarn you like to
do needle point. However, a multi-strand embroidery floss is
recommended since you can pull it apart as needed for thinner
stands.

If you have a hard time threading the needle, insert the tip of the
thread into your mouth and wet it with your saliva. This will stiffen
the thread and make it easier to push through the eye of the needle.

Tip: Make sure to select a needle that you can insert all the way
through your canvas with ease. Check to see if the manufacturer has
recommended a needle size on the canvas label.

5

Secure the thread to the canvas with a waste knot. Tie the knot near the end of the long piece of thread. Then, insert the needle into the canvas on the right (front) side about 1 in (2.5 cm) from where you want to begin stitching. Then, bring the needle back out through the wrong (back) side of the fabric where you want to create the first stitch.[3]

Make sure that you attach the waste knot in the same row that you want to start stitching.

You will cut the waste knot after you stitch over the area around it, so don't worry about it being visible.

Part 2 of 3:
Working Basic Stitches

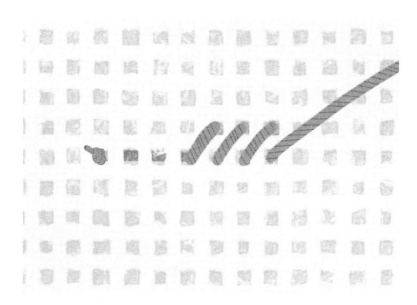

1

Do a half-cross stitch for a simple stitch that covers a small area. Insert the needle through the wrong (back) side of the canvas. Choose a space at the top left of your canvas or at the top left of a block of color. Bring the needle through a space on the right (front) side of the canvas that is diagonally-adjacent to the stitch on the right side. Then, repeat the same stitch to create a stitch alongside your first stitch.[4]

Work from left to right in a row across the canvas, and then work the stitch back along the row in the opposite direction.

As you sew the second row, the second diagonal stitch should go through a space that already has thread going through it. This will help to reduce the visible canvas behind the thread.

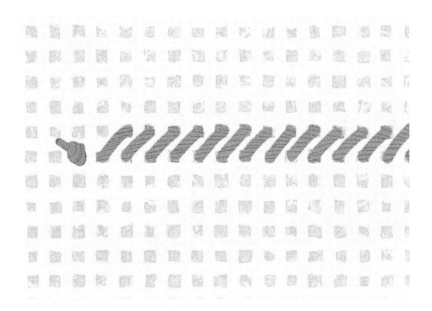

2

Use the continental stitch to provide more coverage over an area. Insert the needle into the space where you want to begin working the continental stitch. Then, bring the needle up diagonally and down through the stitch adjacent and to the right of that stitch. Then, come up through the next space in the row beside where you started the stitch.[5]

Continue to work across the row going from right to left. Then, work back along the next row going from left to right.

Make sure to insert the needle through spaces that already have 1 stitch in them on your second row.

Tip: The continental stitch is very similar to the half-cross stitch, except you work it going from right to left instead of left to right.

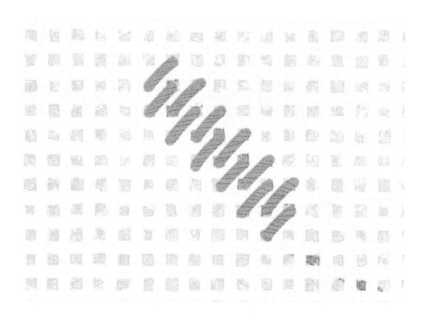

3

Try basketweave stitch to provide full coverage over large areas. Work this stitch diagonally starting at the top right hand corner of the area. Bring the needle down through the space that is diagonal to this space. Then, bring the needle back up through the space that is diagonally adjacent to this stitch, and repeat the stitch.[6]

This stitch creates a pyramid like stitch design. It allows good coverage of the canvas with the least distortion and should be used in large areas.

4

Do the brick stitch for a vertical stitch with good coverage. Insert your needle through the canvas where you want to begin the stitch. Bring the thread all the way through the canvas and pull it taut. Then, insert the needle into the second stitch up from where you brought the needle out. Bring the needle back through the canvas next to where you started the first stitch.[7]

Use a thick thread, yarn, or multi-strand piece of embroidery floss to create the brick stitch.

You can also try the Bargello or long point stitch for a more advanced vertical stitch.[8]

Part 3 of 3:

Completing a Project

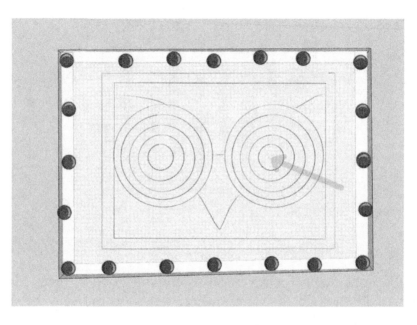

1

Work on the smallest or most detailed area first. Always start with the smallest, most detailed areas when you do needlework projects. This will be easier than trying to go in and stitch those areas later. Then, stitch the larger areas that surround the more detailed bits.

For example, if you have a section that is only about 1 in (2.5 cm) wide, start here rather than the section that is 4 in (10 cm) wide.

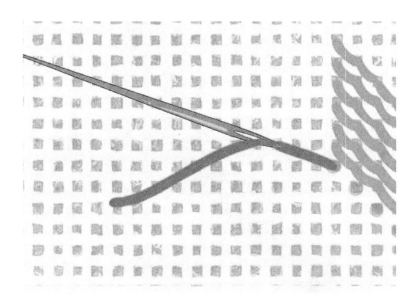

2

Change the thread when you run out or need to switch colors. Insert the needle into the right side of the project. Then, push the needle through the back of the nearest 3 to 4 stitches and snip the thread near the stitches. Then, thread your needle with your next color or with the same color if you have more of this that you need to work. Create a waste knot, and keep stitching![9]

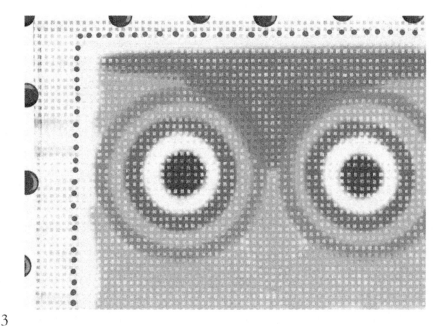

3

Block the canvas if it has become distorted. Blocking your needlepoint is a way to reshape the canvas and give it a more structured look. Remove the canvas from the frame and dampen it with water, such as by spritzing it with a spray bottle. Then, lay it on a pillow or towel with the right side facing down. Pin it down with tacks or pins at 1 in (2.5 cm) intervals all the way around. Allow the canvas to dry completely before removing it.

The canvas should take only a few hours to dry, but you may want to leave it out overnight to be sure.

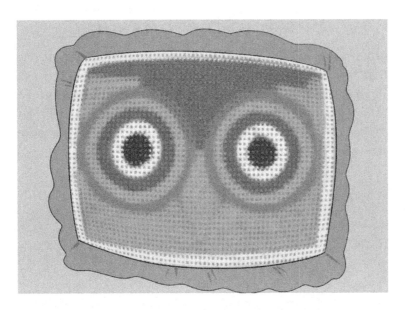

4

Sew the finished design onto an item. You can turn your finished needlework into a pillow, sweatshirt, purse, or wall decoration. Trim the canvas as needed and then use a sewing machine or needle and thread to sew the canvas onto your item.[10]

For example, you could sew your finished needlework project onto a pillowcase, a sweatshirt, or the side of a canvas bag.

How to Work the Bargello or Long Stitch in Needlepoint

The Bargello stitch, also known as the long stitch, is a simple cross stitch that is worked vertically across a canvas to produce a colorful wave-like design. The peaks of this design can be worked so that they appear sharp or soft. People started using this design during the 15th century for tapestries, but it is versatile.[1] Try using the Bargello stitch for your next cross stitch project to get dramatic colorful results.

Part
1
Planning Your Project

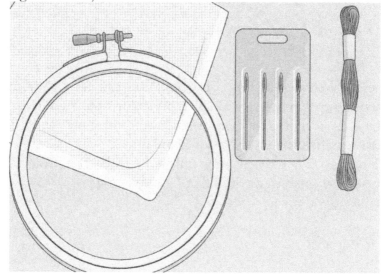

1
Gather your materials. Working the Bargello stitch requires the same basic materials that you need to do other needlecraft stitches. You will need:[2]

Embroidery floss. It is best to opt for a thicker floss, but otherwise you can choose the color and type of floss that best suits your project. You can also use yarn if you are working on a plastic canvas, but yarn is not appropriate for a cloth canvas.

Canvas. You can use a cloth canvas if you will be using embroidery floss or a plastic canvas if you will be using yarn.

Embroidery hoop. This is only necessary if you will be working with a cloth canvas. You can skip the hoop if you are using a plastic canvas.

Tapestry needle. Make sure the eye of the needle is large enough to fit your thread or yarn through.

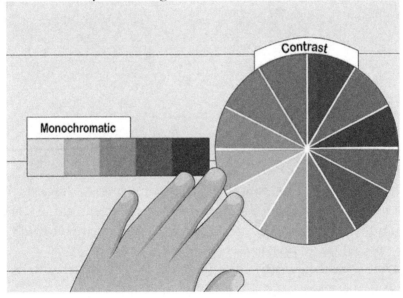

2

Consider your color scheme. Bargello stitch looks best when you use a variety of different colors to create your designs. In general, the two types of color schemes that people use for the Bargello stitch include:[3]

Monochromatic. This means that the colors are all different shades of the same color. For example, you might begin with a dark blue, then switch to a medium blue, then a light blue, and then a pale baby blue. Contrasting. These are colors that are across from each other on the color wheel, such as yellow and purple or red and green.

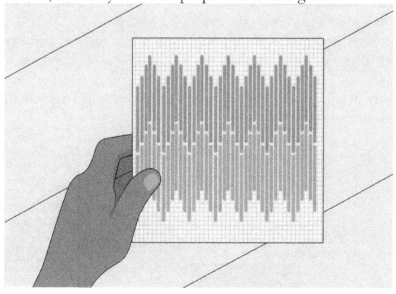

3

Choose or design a pattern. You can find pre-made Bargello stitch patterns to follow, or you can just use a basic Bargello stitch to create a design. If you want to create a custom design, then you could even draw one out on graph paper.

To create your own design using the basic Bargello stitch, use colored pencils to mark spaces on a piece of graph paper.

The Bargello stitch can be worked over two to six canvas spaces, but the stitches are always vertical or horizontal.

The stitches occur in gradations that create the appearance of waves or sharp peaks depending on how far apart your space them.

Part
2
Working a Basic Bargello or Long Stitch

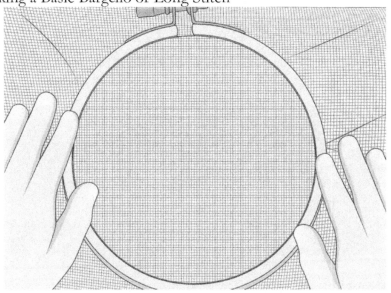

1
Mount your canvas in an embroidery hoop. Start by placing your canvas in an embroidery hoop and securing it in place. This will help to ensure that you have a taut surface to embroider, which will make your work much easier.

The only exception is if you are using plastic canvas with yarn. In this case, you do not need to use an embroidery hoop because the plastic canvas is thick enough to hold its shape.

2

Insert your thread through the first hole in your pattern. When you are ready to begin working the Bargello stitch, thread your tapestry needle with an 18 inch (46 cm) strand of embroidery floss. Then, insert the needle going through the back of the canvas and into the top part of the first stitch.[4]

Make sure to tie a knot in the end of your strand of thread to anchor it to the back of the first stitch. Otherwise, your thread will pull right through the hole.

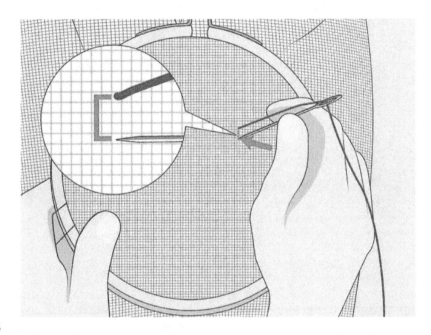

3

Bring the thread down to the end point of the stitch. Next, pull the thread through until it is anchored by the knot and then bring the thread down towards the end point of your first stitch. Keep in mind that a Bargello stitch may cross over two to six canvas spaces to create each stitch.[5]

For example, if you started your stitch in the top corner space of your canvas, then you might bring the needle down and through the fourth space from the top of the canvas in the same row.

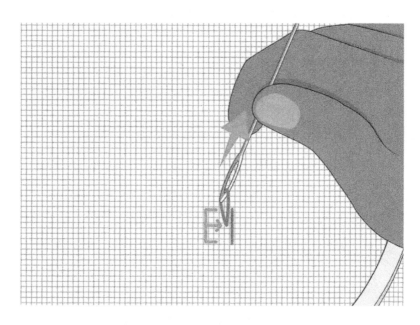

4

Go up through your next stitch. Next, you will need to make an upward stitch. Insert your needle through the back of your canvas where you want the bottom of your next stitch to be. The location of this next stitch will depend on how sharp or soft you want your peaks to be.[6]

If you want to create a sharp peak for your next stitch, then you would insert the needle through a space in the next row that is near the center of your first stitch or two or more spaces above it.

If you want to create a soft peak or wave-like design, then you would insert the needle so that it comes out only one space above or below your first stitch.

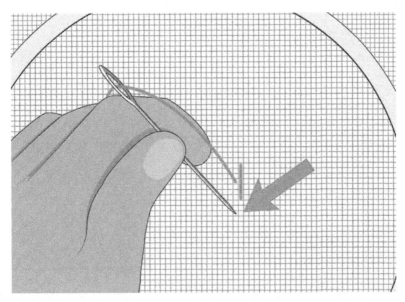

5

Bring the thread up to the next endpoint. After you bring your thread up through the canvas again, pull the thread up and across the spaces and bring it down through the endpoint for that stitch. Make sure that the stitch covers the same amount of canvas spaces as your first stitch even though the stitch will have shifted up or down.[7]

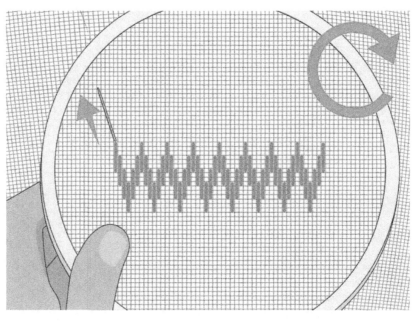

6

Continue to stitch up and down until you complete your pattern. You will need to start the process over again after you complete your second stitch. Keep repeating this stitch sequence and moving the locations of your stitches according to your design until you have completed your project.[8]

Part
3
Getting the Best Results

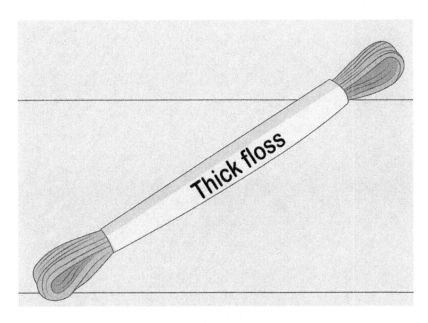

1

Choose a thick floss. Since the Bargello stitch covers multiple canvas spaces, a thick floss is best. A thick floss will make it easier to cover the surface area of your canvas. If you do not have a thick floss, then combine two or three strands of the floss you do have to ensure good coverage of the canvas.[9]

If you are working with a multi-ply thread, such as Watercolors, then you will need to separate the threads and then regroup them together before using the thread. This will help to increase the surface coverage and ensure that the threads lay flat.

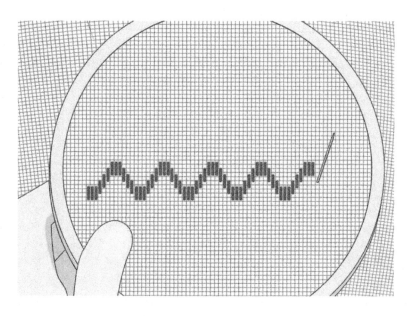

2

Use spacing to change the appearance of the design. As you plan out your Bargello stitch design, keep in mind that the amount of space between your stitches will affect the way that the completed design looks. Adding more vertical space between the stitches will result in sharper peaks while keeping your stitches closer together will result in softer peaks that look like waves.[10]

For extra soft peaks, you can even try putting two or three stitches parallel with each other in the valleys of your design.

3

Avoid working too close to another design. The Bargello stitch is striking and it can be overwhelming when placed alongside other designs. Therefore, it is best to avoid placing Bargello stitches right next to other design elements. If you want to use Bargello stitch to frame another design, such as a cross stitch animal, then surround the design with some basic cross stitching. This will form a cushion between the design and the Bargello stitches.

9 Beginner Needlepoint Basics to Get You Started

01
of 09
What Is Needlepoint? Definition and Brief History Explained

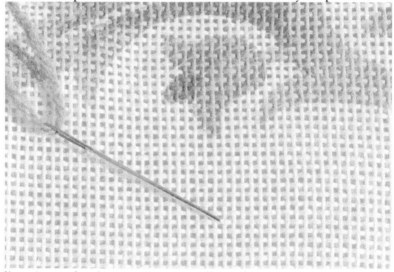

Needlepoint is both creative as well as therapeutic; it engages both the hands as well as the imagination, causing the body to relax and de-stress with the simple gentle rhythm of thread working through the canvas.

Worked in stitch techniques designed specifically for needlepoint, a project can be made with a graph or chart by counting squares and making stitches from them onto canvas; or by filling in a design that has already been painted on the canvas itself.

Needlepoint has been worked for centuries around the world. Learn more about the history of needlepoint and how it differs from other forms of embroidery.

02
of 09
Needlepoint Canvas Facts Every Beginner Should Know

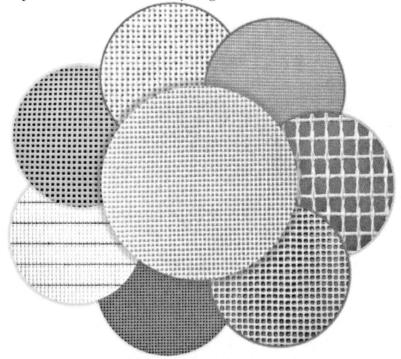

Needlepoint canvas is the ground fabric used to work a project. It comes in a variety of sizes--from very fine canvas that looks like gauze to the traditional coarse crisp fabric. Gain a better understanding of the canvas used to make needlepoint projects in this Ultimate Guide.

Learn about the various types of even-weave needlepoint canvas--

from basic to novelty, as well as the perfect size canvas you should use for your first beginner needlepoint project.

03
of 09
Basic Tent Needlepoint Stitches to Get You Started

Tent Stitches are the basic foundation stitches of most needlepoint projects and are also a family of stitches worked diagonally on the canvas. Most diagonal needlepoint stitches are derived from one or all three of the traditional tent stitches.

This easy-to-follow Needlepoint Wiki will show you how to work the three basic tent stitches: Half-Cross, Continental and Basketweave. Included are instructions for right and left-handed beginners as well.

04
of 09
Needlepoint Thread Basics

Not all yarn or thread is suitable for needlepoint, but there are hundreds of fibers that can be used to stitch a needlepoint design. Find out the best yarn and thread types to use in working a beginner needlepoint project.

Learn about textured fibers and novelty needlepoint yarns to use in accenting a specific area of a needlepoint design.

05
of 09
Choosing the Right Needle for Needlepoint

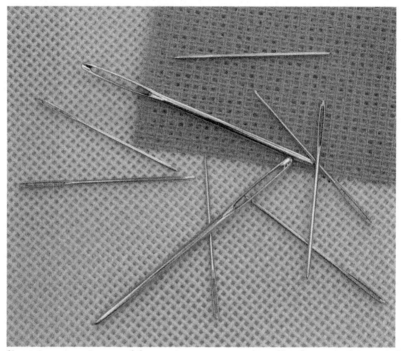

Needlepoint requires a blunt tip tapestry needle for stitching. These needles come in a variety of sizes.

Get tips on the right size needed to work your project as well as different ways to easily and properly thread the needle to make your needlepoint stitches look smooth and even.

06
of 09
Needlepoint Tools and Supplies

Needlepoint requires only a few basic inexpensive tools. Check out these tips for MUST HAVE and WISHLIST items every needle pointer should keep on hand.

Start with the basics like canvas, tapestry needles, yarn and thread; and then as you gain more experience working needlepoint projects, gradually add frames, stretcher bars, and other convenient items to your collection.

07
of 09

Althea DeBrule
Here are suggestions as well as a step-by-step tutorial on how to download, enlarge and print needlepoint patterns and charts found online.

You'll learn how to save them to your computer for easy access and to re-use them in other needlepoint projects.

08
of 09
Step-by-Step Instructions for Working a Waste Knot

To begin stitching a needlepoint project requires that you use a waste or away knot. This not sits on top of the canvas to allow the threads to be properly secured on the back.

With these simple instructions, you can learn how to easily make an Away or Waste Knot to get ready for smooth and even stitching.

Continue to 9 of 9 below.

09
of 09
Blocking and Finishing a Needlepoint Project

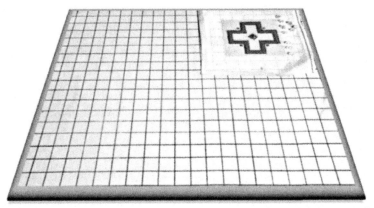

A first needlepoint project, when completed, will most often be slightly warped and a little out of shape. You can easily square up your finished project with a blocking board and a few simple instructions.

Learn how easy it is to do-it-yourself and block your needlepoint to restore the canvas to its original sizing and shape

Printed in Great Britain
by Amazon

42284351R00030